W9-AFZ-882

# DC COMICS
# SUPER HEROES

# HEROIC MISSIONS

## WRITTEN BY SIMON HUGO AND CAVAN SCOTT

# INTRODUCTION

The LEGO® DC™ Super Heroes use their amazing powers to keep the universe safe. When danger comes to call, this team of heroes are always ready to face it head-on.

## HOW TO USE THIS BOOK

This books is a guide to awesome LEGO DC minifigures. These amazing minifigures are ordered chronologically according to when they were first released.

# CONTENTS

# SUPERMAN
## THE MAN OF STEEL

## VITAL STATS
................................

**LIKES:** A peaceful Metropolis
**DISLIKES:** Kryptonite
**FRIENDS:** Wonder Woman,
Lois Lane
**FOES:** Lex Luthor
**SKILLS:** Heat vision
**GEAR:** Cape

**SET NAMES:** Superman
(NYCC 2011 exclusive),
Superman vs Power Armor Lex
**SET NUMBERS:**
COMCON017, 6862
**YEARS:** 2011, 2012

A determined face:
Superman is ready
to stand for truth
and justice.

Eye-catching
red cape

## DEFENDER OF METROPOLIS

On the other side of his double-
sided face, Superman wears a
confident smile—the Kryptonian
enjoys banishing alien threats
from his hometown, Metropolis.

Superman's
yellow belt is
also printed
on his back.

**The last survivor** of the doomed
planet Krypton, Superman was
rocketed to Earth as a baby.
Powered by the sun, the Man of
Steel can fly faster than a speeding
bullet, lift incredible weights, and
fire lasers from his eyes.

# WONDER WOMAN
## AMAZONIAN PRINCESS

### VITAL STATS
..........................

**LIKES:** Honesty
**DISLIKES:** Lies
**FRIENDS:** Superman
**FOES:** Lex Luthor
**SKILLS:** Advanced fighting techniques
**GEAR:** Lasso of Truth

**SET NAME:** Superman vs Power Armor Lex
**SET NUMBER:** 6862
**YEAR:** 2012

The minifigure's hairpiece includes Wonder Woman's golden tiara.

Wonder Woman's costume is based upon the flag of the United States of America.

### FORCING THE TRUTH
No one can lie once they're tangled in Wonder Woman's Lasso of Truth. A turn of her head shows how angry she was to be captured by Lex Luthor.

**Born on Paradise Island,** Amazonian Princess Diana trained to be a warrior from the moment she could fight. The strongest woman on the planet, she now fights crime as a member of the Justice League.

# SHAZAM!
## THE WORLD'S MIGHTIEST MORTAL

## VITAL STATS

**LIKES:** Being a hero
**DISLIKES:** Being a kid
**FRIENDS:** The Justice League
**FOES:** Black Adam
**SKILLS:** Magical abilities
**GEAR:** White cape

**SET NAME:** Shazam
(SDCC 2012 exclusive)
**SET NUMBER:** COMCON020
**YEAR:** 2012

### DID YOU KNOW?
Shazam appears in the LEGO® Batman™ 2: DC Comics Super Heroes and LEGO Batman 3: Beyond Gotham video games.

Shazam shares a hairpiece with Bruce Wayne

Printed body emblazoned with lightning strike

Shazam wears one of the longest capes to appear on a LEGO® DC Comics Super Heroes minifigure.

### RAGE AND FURY
Shazam uses his great wisdom to think his way out of trouble. That doesn't means he always remains calm. The other side of Shazam's head shows him shouting in anger.

**Aged ten, Billy Batson** was granted magical powers by a wizard. By shouting "Shazam!" Billy changes into a powerful being blessed with the ability of legendary heroes Solomon, Hercules, Atlas, Zeus, Achilles, and Mercury (spelling "Shazam").

# JOR-EL
## SUPERMAN'S FATHER

### VITAL STATS

**LIKES:** Science
**DISLIKES:** The Kryptonian Council
**FRIENDS:** His wife Lara
**FOES:** General Zod
**SKILLS:** Code imprinting
**GEAR:** Dark brown cape

**SET NAME:** Jor-El (polybag)
**SET NUMBER:** 5001623
**YEAR:** 2013

### DID YOU KNOW?

This minifigure is based on the 2013 *Man of Steel* movie. It was given free to customers at shop.LEGO.com and LEGO stores in June 2013.

Armor detailing is similar to Superman's *Man of Steel* variant

The "S" symbol means "hope" in Kryptonian.

### FROM FATHER TO SON

As "Clark Kent", Superman discovered a Kryptonian spaceship on Earth. From it, a holographic image of Jor-El appeared to teach Clark about his alien heritage and present the Last Son of Krypton with his Superman uniform.

While Superman's armor is gold in tones, Jor-El's is bronze.

**When chief scientist** Jor-El realized that his planet Krypton was about to explode, he tried to warn the Kryptonian High Council. With Jor-El's advice going ignored, he sent his son to Earth for safety. This son would become Superman!

# AQUAMAN
## RULER OF ATLANTIS

## VITAL STATS
..........................

**LIKES:** The ocean
**DISLIKES:** Ice prisons
**FRIENDS:** Batman
**FOES:** Mr. Freeze
**SKILLS:** Controlling sea-life
**GEAR:** Golden trident

**SET NAMES:** Arctic Batman
vs. Mr Freeze: Aquaman
on Ice, Black Manta Deep
Sea Strike
**SET NUMBERS:** 76000,
76027
**YEARS:** 2013, 2015

An angry face as
Aquaman plans a
retaliation attack

Aquaman can
blast water out
of his trident.

Aquaman's muscles are
also printed on the
back of the minifigure.

### FROZEN FISH
The marine minifigure's
reversible head shows a more
somber expression. Aquaman
had plenty of time to think
when he was put on ice in Mr.
Freeze's petrifying polar prison.

**Half–human and half–Atlantean,**
Aquaman tirelessly defends Earth's
oceans from attack. The briny ruler
is able to communicate telepathically
with fish and sea mammals, and was
one of the founding members of the
Justice League.

# GREEN ARROW
## THE EMERALD ARCHER

## VITAL STATS

**LIKES:** Hitting the bull's-eye
**DISLIKES:** Commitment
**FRIENDS:** The Justice League
**FOES:** Merlyn
**SKILLS:** Archery
**GEAR:** Green hood

**SET NAME:** Green Arrow
(SDCC 2013 exclusive)
**SET NUMBER:** COMCON030
**YEAR:** 2013

Green hood

**DID YOU KNOW?**
This is the only LEGO DC Comics Super Heroes Green Arrow minifigure not to have a bow and arrow!

Cool Super Hero stubble

Arrow insignia on belt

## TWO'S COMPANY

This rare Green Arrow kept company with black-suited Superman at the 2013 San Diego Comic-Con.

Kneepads printed on legs

**Another Comic-Con** exclusive, 200 Green Arrow minifigures were offered up for raffle in July 2013. They are based on Green Arrow's updated 2011 costume from the comics. Previously, Green Arrow had sported a yellow goatee.

# LOIS LANE
## DAILY PLANET REPORTER

## VITAL STATS
................................

**LIKES:** Following leads
**DISLIKES:** Being kidnapped
**FRIENDS:** Superman
**FOES:** General Zod
**SKILLS:** Investigating,
escaping from aliens
**GEAR:** Wits and bravery

**SET NAMES:** Superman: Black
Zero escape
**SET NUMBERS:** 76009
**YEARS:** 2013

### DID YOU KNOW?
This Lois Lane
minifigure is based on her
appearance in the 2013
*Man of Steel* movie.

Lois shares
her long red
hair with
eight other
minifigures.

Exclusive head
only available on
this minifigure

Printed blouse and
vest is suitable attire
for a newshound

## ESCAPE POD PERIL
Is it any wonder the other side
of Lois' head has a terrified
expression? She's been thrown
out of General Zod's Black Zero
ship in an escape pod!

Practical blue
pants

**Intrepid reporter** Lois Lane knew
she had a story on her hands from
the moment the first reports about
Superman came in. Following her
leads, she tracked the Man of Steel
to his Smallville home and
discovered his secret identity.

# SUPERMAN
## LAST SON OF KRYPTON

### VITAL STATS

**LIKES:** Metropolis
**DISLIKES:** Falling structures
**FRIENDS:** Lois Lane, Jimmy Olsen
**FOES:** General Zod
**SKILLS:** Heat vision
**GEAR:** Red cape

**SET NAMES:** Superman: Metropolis Showdown, Superman: Battle of Smallville, Superman: Black Zero Escape
**SET NUMBERS:** 76002, 76003, 76009
**YEAR:** 2013

Peek beneath the cape and you'll see Superman's suit also printed on the back of the minifigure.

Silver armor detailing, as befits a battle-ready suit

Details of the suit are also printed on the legs.

### TURNING UP THE HEAT

One side of Superman's head shows an angry expression and red eyes as he fights to save Metropolis and Smallville from the villainous Zod. The other side wears a calmer frown.

**Darker than the** classic Superman outfit, this more modern-looking Man of Steel has rid himself of the red pants over his tights. This suit is modeled on traditional Kryptonian clothing, worn under battle armor on Superman's home planet.

# OFFROADER
## BIG IN SMALLVILLE

### VITAL STATS

**OWNER:** Colonel Hardy
**USED FOR:** Ground-to-air defense
**GEAR:** Missile launcher

**SET NAME:** Superman: Battle of Smallville
**SET NUMBER:** 76003
**YEAR:** 2013

**DID YOU KNOW?**
Brick-yellow pieces such as the Offroader's cabin, were first seen in the LEGO® Adventurers theme in 1998.

Flick-fire missiles

Rocket launcher can rotate by 360 degrees

Cabin with two seats is one piece

### HARDY DEFENSE
Brave Colonel Hardy knows his Offroader's missile launcher is no match for General Zod's Black Zero Dropship, but he still uses it to defend Smallville when the Kryptonian criminal attacks.

Chunky all-terrain tires

**This sand-colored** utility vehicle is equipped for battle, with searchlights and a pair of rocket launchers mounted on the back. It can seat two U.S. Air Force soldiers, and is driven by Colonel Hardy when the town of Smallville comes under attack.

# COLONEL HARDY
## U.S. AIR FORCE HERO

## VITAL STATS

**LIKES:** United States Air Force
**DISLIKES:** Helicopters
**FRIENDS:** Superman, Lois Lane
**FOES:** General Zod, Faora
**SKILLS:** Pilot
**GEAR:** Gun

**SET NAME:** Superman: Battle of Smallville
**SET NUMBER:** 76003
**YEAR:** 2013

Bald head for this bold hero

Pockets to store ammo

Radio to call for back up

### DID YOU KNOW?
Colonel Hardy shares a head with the Bank Guard from The Batmobile and the Two-Face Chase (set 8684).

### GETTING THE DROP ON ZOD
Colonel Hardy becomes a hero when he stages an attack on Zod's spacecraft. He triggers a portal that drags the ship back to the Phantom Zone proving that the mighty Dropship is no match for the nifty offroader.

**A member of the** U.S. Air Force, Colonel Nathan Hardy was ordered to bring down the battling Kryptonians that were flattening Smallville. However, the Colonel realized that the Man of Steel wasn't their enemy after Superman saved his life.

# THE FLASH
## THE FASTEST MAN ALIVE

Remove the helmet to find a two-sided face complete with a red mask surround.

Flip the head to reveal an angry expression

Exclusive helmet with yellow bolts on each side

Costume printing continues onto the back of the minifigure

Flash insignia

## THE NEED FOR SPEED

The Flash was on hand to help Batman chase down the Riddler's dragster. With his acrobatic abilities he jumps over the Riddler's bombs (and bananas), and remains in hot pursuit of the questionable criminal.

## DID YOU KNOW?

The Flash appears in the LEGO *Batman 2: DC Comics Super Heroes* and LEGO *Batman 3: Beyond Gotham* video games.

**After he was struck** by lightning, police scientist Barry Allen developed the power to run at high speeds. Able to outrun anything on the planet, The Flash rushed into a life fighting crime and was one of the founding members of the Justice League.

# SUPERBOY
## THE BOY OF STEEL

### DID YOU KNOW?
Superboy's first LEGO appearance was in the videogame LEGO *Batman 2: DC Super Heroes*, where he wore an all-black outfit.

Same tousled hair as Robin

Muscle tone shows through tight shirt

Rare two-tone minifigure arms gives t-shirt effect

### A LIKELY LAD
In 2015 exclusive set 5004077 revealed another Super Hero from faraway: Lightning Lad. This character's ability to create eletricity is shown with the dramatic lightning bolts on his minifigure's torso and legs.

Blue jeans show Superboy's casual approach to costumes!

**Conner Kent** was cloned from Lex Luthor and Superman's DNA, but still became Superman's pal, earning the Kryptonian name Kon-El. He has similar abilities to Superman, such as super strength, heat vision, x-ray vision, freeze breath, and flight.

# GREEN LANTERN
## GUARDIAN OF EARTH

## VITAL STATS

**LIKES:** Protecting the Earth
**DISLIKES:** Losing his Lantern
**FRIENDS:** Batman
**FOES:** Sinestro
**SKILLS:** Space flight
**GEAR:** Green Lantern

**SET NAME:** Green Lantern
vs. Sinestro
**SET NUMBER:** 76025
**YEAR:** 2015

Green Lantern shares a hairpiece with Commissioner Gordon.

A two-sided head features a grinning face on the reverse

Green Lantern uniform complete with the insignia of the Lantern Corps

### DOWN-TO-EARTH
An earlier Green Lantern, based on the 2011 *Green Lantern* movie, was given away to 1,500 raffle winners at the 2011 San Diego Comic-Con, with a smaller quantity released at New York Comic Con the same year.

Black and green printing continues on the back

**When test pilot** Hal Jordan discovered the wreckage of an alien spacecraft he received a power ring that transformed him into the Green Lantern. Drawing power from his cosmic lantern, Hal protects the solar system from attack.

# CONSTRUCT SPACESHIP
## IMAGINE THAT!

## VITAL STATS

**OWNER:** Green Lantern
**USED FOR:** Visiting other planets
**GEAR:** Shooters, ultra-fast engine

**SET NAME:** Green Lantern vs. Sinestro
**SET NUMBER:** 76025
**YEAR:** 2015

### DID YOU KNOW?
Green Lantern can use his power ring to make solid constructs of anything he imagines—not just spaceships!

Shooters on both wings

Forward shooters

### A GIANT LEAP...
The Green Lantern vs. Sinestro set also comes with a special Super Jumper piece that serves as a springboard for minifigures to perform giant leaps.

**Made from energy** channeled through a power ring, this spaceship only works while Green Lantern is concentrating! Hal Jordan creates it to chase after Sinestro, when the villain steals his Power Battery and takes it to the planet Korugar.

# WONDER WOMAN
## AMAZONIAN WARRIOR

### VITAL STATS

**LIKES:** Making a monkey of villains
**DISLIKES:** Bananas
**FRIENDS:** Batman, The Flash
**FOES:** Gorilla Grodd, Captain Cold
**SKILLS:** Piloting invisible jet planes
**GEAR:** Swords

**SET NAME:** Gorilla Grodd Goes Bananas
**SET NUMBER:** 76026
**YEAR:** 2015

Face printing appears in six other sets

Silver tiara

New battle-ready uniform exclusive to set

### SWORD HELD HIGH

A twist of Wonder Woman's head reveals her scowling as she rushes into the fray, armed with her Amazonian sword. She's a foe to be reckoned with thanks to a lifetime of combat training.

Pants replace her satin tights

**Fighting crime in a** modern age, the new Wonder Woman is based on an updated costume first introduced to the comics in 2011. Her armor is also printed on the back of her minifigure. Villains beware, this Wonder Woman is ready for battle.

# INVISIBLE JET
## NOTHING TO SEE HERE!

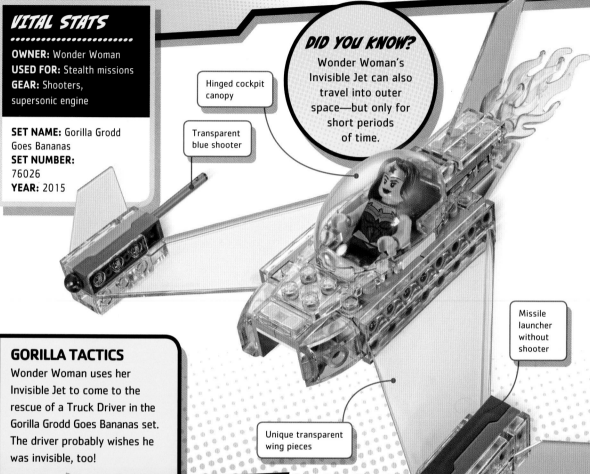

## VITAL STATS
......................

**OWNER:** Wonder Woman
**USED FOR:** Stealth missions
**GEAR:** Shooters,
supersonic engine

**SET NAME:** Gorilla Grodd
Goes Bananas
**SET NUMBER:**
76026
**YEAR:** 2015

### DID YOU KNOW?
Wonder Woman's
Invisible Jet can also
travel into outer
space—but only for
short periods
of time.

Hinged cockpit
canopy

Transparent
blue shooter

Missile
launcher
without
shooter

Unique transparent
wing pieces

## GORILLA TACTICS
Wonder Woman uses her
Invisible Jet to come to the
rescue of a Truck Driver in the
Gorilla Grodd Goes Bananas set.
The driver probably wishes he
was invisible, too!

**Wonder Woman built** the
Invisible Jet in the name of peace.
By traveling unseen, she can carry
out her missions without starting
a fight. The plane is super-fast and
a complete stealth vehicle. Even
the exhaust flames are invisible!

GOING BANANAS

In Gorilla Grodd Goes Bananas (set 76026), the oversized "bigfig" Gorilla Grodd causes chaos, Wonder Woman debuts her Invisible Jet, and Batman takes the high ground in his Bat-Mech.

# TRUCK DRIVER
## DRIVEN AROUND THE BEND

Terrified expression

Back printing shows that this driver works for "Banana Co."

Happy banana logo

Practical dungarees

## A BAD DAY AT WORK

First his truck is raided, then he's swung upside-down by a very hungry Grodd! It's shaping up to be a bad day for the truck driver. Frequent super-villain attacks mean there are lots of job vacancies in Gotham City as workers flee from danger.

**Talk about being** in the wrong place at the wrong time. All the Truck Driver had to do was deliver a batch of bright yellow bananas to Gotham City's fruit lovers. Easy—unless you run into a giant hyper-intelligent gorilla.

# GREEN ARROW
## ANGRY ARCHER

## VITAL STATS

**LIKES:** Shooting straight
**DISLIKES:** A close shave
**FRIENDS:** Superman, Cyborg
**FOES:** Darkseid
**SKILLS:** Archery
**GEAR:** Longbow

**SET NAMES:** Darkseid Invasion
**SET NUMBERS:** 76028
**YEARS:** 2015

Face stubble printing reveals that the Green Archer is in need of a shave

Green plastic hood hangs from around the neck

## ARMED AND DANGEROUS

You can swivel the Green Arrow's head to reveal an angry expression. A quiver full of arrows is also printed on the back of his torso, beneath his cape.

Standard LEGO bow and arrow in green

**With a body similar** to the earlier San Diego Comic-Con exclusive, this Green Arrow has plain green legs rather than kneepads. Luckily for the Justice League, the Arrow stays on target no matter what his workday wardrobe.

# THE JAVELIN
## THE JUSTIC LEAGUE'S SPACESHIP

## VITAL STATS

**OWNER:** Green Arrow
**USED FOR:** Justice League missions
**GEAR:** Bombs, rockets

**SET NAMES:** Darkseid Invasion
**SET NUMBERS:** 76028
**YEARS:** 2015

### DID YOU KNOW?
Darkseid Invasion was the first set to include a springy Super Jumper element—hidden in the Javelin's cargo bay.

Double doors open to reveal large cargo bay

Justice League emblem on nose cone

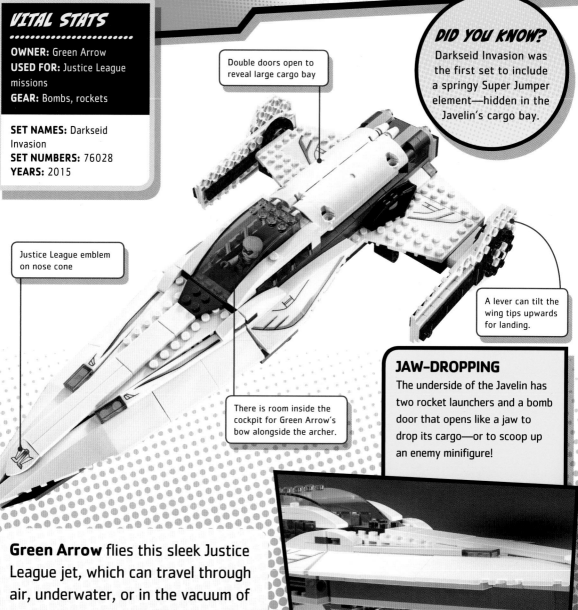

A lever can tilt the wing tips upwards for landing.

There is room inside the cockpit for Green Arrow's bow alongside the archer.

### JAW-DROPPING
The underside of the Javelin has two rocket launchers and a bomb door that opens like a jaw to drop its cargo—or to scoop up an enemy minifigure!

**Green Arrow** flies this sleek Justice League jet, which can travel through air, underwater, or in the vacuum of space. It was built by Batman and is equipped with all the gadgets and gear you'd expect from him—just not in his usual dark color scheme!

# HAWKMAN
## WINGED WARRIOR

## VITAL STATS

**LIKES:** Flying high
**DISLIKES:** Having his wings clipped
**FRIENDS:** Superman, Cyborg, Green Arrow
**FOES:** Darkseid
**SKILLS:** Flight
**GEAR:** Wings, Mace

**SET NAMES:** Darkseid Invasion
**SET NUMBERS:** 76028
**YEARS:** 2015

Golden helmet also winged to be aerodynamic

Wings attach to Hawkman's minifigure using gold studs.

Hawk symbol joins crossing chest straps

### BEATING WINGS

Hawkman comes with two interchangeable set of plastic wings, one spread out for flight and the other drawn in for fight! There's also a two-sided head beneath that helmet.

**Archaeologist Carter Hall** uses magical Nth Metal to soar through the air as the savage Hawkman. This Justice League member is no young featherweight—he's actually a reincarnated Egyptian prince!

**Project Editor** Emma Grange
**Editors** Tina Jindal, Matt Jones, Clare Millar, Rosie Peet
**Senior Designers** Nathan Martin, Mark Penfound,
David McDonald
**Designers** Karan Chaudhary, Stefan Georgiou
**Pre-Production Producer** Kavita Varma
**Senior Producer** Lloyd Robertson
**Managing Editors** Paula Regan,
Chitra Subramanyam
**Design Managers** Neha Ahuja, Guy Harvey
**Creative Manager** Sarah Harland
**Art Director** Lisa Lanzarini
**Publisher** Julie Ferris
**Publishing Director** Simon Beecroft

**Additional Photography** Markos Chouris,
Christopher Chouris, Gary Ombler

First American Edition, 2016
Published in the United States by DK Publishing
345 Hudson Street, New York, NY 10014
DK, a Division of Penguin Random House LLC

001–298875–Jul/16

Contains content previously published in LEGO® DC Comics™
Super Heroes Character Encyclopedia (2016)

Page design Copyright © 2016 Dorling Kindersley Limited

A catalog record for this book is available from
the Library of Congress.

ISBN: 978-5-0010-1412-6

Printed and bound in China

www.LEGO.com
www.dk.com
A WORLD OF IDEAS:
SEE ALL THERE IS TO KNOW

## ACKNOWLEDGMENTS
DK would like to thank Randi Sørensen,
Paul Hansford, Martin Leighton Lindhardt, Maria
Bloksgaard Markussen, Adam Corbally, Daniel
Mckenna, Casper Glahder, Adam Siegmund Grabowski,
John Cuppage, Justin Ramsden, Karl Oskar Jonas
Norlen, Marcos Bessa, Sally Aston, Sven Robin Kahl,
and Mauricio Bedolla at the LEGO Group, Ben Harper,
Thomas Zellers, and Melanie Swartz at Warner Bros.,
Cavan Scott and Simon Hugo for their writing,
and Sam Bartlett for design assistance.